ERIC WILLIAM GILMOUR

Mary of Bethany

"WHAT SHE HAS DONE WILL BE TOLD, IN MEMORY OF HER."

Copyright © Eric William Gilmour

All rights reserved. No part of this book may be used or reproduced by any means, graphic, electronic, mechanical, including photocopying, recording, taping, or by any information storage retrieval system without the written permission of the author except in the case of brief quotations embodied in critical articles and reviews.

All scriptures are quoted in the New American Standard Version of the Bible unless otherwise noted.

New American Standard NEW AMERICAN STANDARD BIBLE Copyright (C) 1960, 1962, 1963, 1968, 1971, 1972, 1973, 1975, 1977,1995 by THE LOCKMAN FOUNDATION A Corporation Not for Profit LA HABRA, CA All Rights Reserved

Scripture quotations marked (NIV) are taken from the Holy Bible, New International Version®, NIV®. Copyright © 1973, 1978, 1984, 2011 by Biblica, Inc.™ Used by permission of Zondervan. All rights reserved worldwide. www.zondervan.com The "NIV" and "New International Version" are trademarks registered in the United States Patent and Trademark Office by Biblica, Inc.™

Pulpit to Page Publishing Co. books may be ordered through booksellers or by contacting:

Pulpit to Page Publishing Co.
Warsaw, Indiana
pulpittopage.com

ISBN: 978-1984162090
ISBN: 1984162098

Library of Congress Control Number: 2018932442

Contents

The Biblical Accounts of Mary of Bethany... 2

Introduction... 7

The **First** Mention of Mary of Bethany... 15

The **Second** Mention of Mary of Bethany... 32

The **Third** Mention of Mary of Bethany... 40

The Biblical Accounts of Mary of Bethany

Before beginning an exposition on such a person, it's only fitting to present you with the biblical accounts of her example. This is Mary of Bethany.

Matthew 26:6-13
"Now when Jesus was in Bethany, at the home of Simon the leper, a woman came to Him with an alabaster vial of very costly perfume, and she poured it on His head as He reclined *at the table*. But the disciples were indignant when they saw *this*, and said, "Why this waste? For this *perfume* might have been sold for a high price and *the money* given to the poor." But Jesus, aware of this, said to them,

"Why do you bother the woman? For she has done a good deed to Me. For you always have the poor with you; but you do not always have Me. For when she poured this perfume on My body, she did it to prepare Me for burial. Truly I say to you, wherever this gospel is preached in the whole world, what this woman has done will also be spoken of in memory of her."

John 12:1-11

"Jesus, therefore, six days before the Passover, came to Bethany where Lazarus was, whom Jesus had raised from the dead. So they made Him a supper there, and Martha was serving; but Lazarus was one of those reclining *at the table* with Him. Mary then took a pound of very costly perfume of pure nard, and anointed the feet of Jesus and wiped His feet with her hair; and the house was filled with the fragrance of the perfume. But Judas Iscariot, one of His disciples, who was intending to betray Him, said, "Why was this perfume not sold for three hundred denarii and given to poor *people*?" Now he said this, not because he was concerned about the poor, but because he was a thief, and as he had the money box, he used to pilfer what was put into it. Therefore Jesus said, "Let her alone, so that she may keep it for the day of My burial. For you always have the poor with you, but you do not always have Me."

The large crowd of the Jews then learned

that He was there; and they came, not for Jesus' sake only, but that they might also see Lazarus, whom He raised from the dead. But the chief priests planned to put Lazarus to death also; because on account of him many of the Jews were going away and were believing in Jesus.

Luke 10:38-42
"Now as they were traveling along, He entered a village; and a woman named Martha welcomed Him into her home. She had a sister called Mary, who was seated at the Lord's feet, listening to His word. But Martha was distracted with all her preparations; and she came up *to Him* and said, "Lord, do You not care that my sister has left me to do all the serving alone? Then tell her to help me."

But the Lord answered and said to her, "Martha, Martha, you are worried and bothered about so many things; but *only* one thing is necessary, for Mary has chosen the good part, which shall not be taken away from her."

Introduction

Rest is the realm of God. The scriptures describe God as *seated*. He is always resting. In fact, Jesus is called our Sabbath. He *is* our rest. In order for us to receive from Him, we must join Him there in that seated posture of rest.

Rest is also the realm of *perception*, and in *perceiving* Him, we are then able to *receive* Him. This is very crucial. Why? So often, people have encounters with God—which is great. They experience a massive outbreak of the Holy Spirit in a meeting, and then a couple weeks later, they return to life as-is. *This* exact tragedy is my burden.

I and many of my friends saw this happen repeatedly when we were at Brownsville. An awesome outbreak of God would occur, and the glory would manifest mightily. We watched people get completely rocked by the Holy Ghost in undeniable ways, yet today many of them don't even believe that God exists. Many have turned away and fallen back into sin. Why would such a tragedy occur? It's simple: the public touch has got to turn into a private kiss—or it will all fade away. The reason He gives a public touch is to draw you to a private kiss.

> *"The reason He gives a public touch is to draw you to a private kiss.*

Have you ever said something to someone in conversation, and suddenly God takes your exact words and throws them back at you? I remember a time when God grabbed words I spoke and spoke them right back to me. I was playing around with my daughter and trying to tackle her before bed. I said playfully, "If you don't let me kiss you, there is no way for you to love me!" I tried again, "Baby, if you don't let me kiss you, there's no way for you to love me!"

God took my words, redirected them, and spoke to me by them: "Eric, if you don't let me kiss you, there's no way for you to love me." What does that mean? You *have* to be touched! You *have* to be kissed! You have to be held! You must know the sweet, intimate touch that takes place behind closed doors! All of the public things are wonderful, but the reason for them is for us to fall in love with Him! Oh, that we would know what it is to go into the King's chamber and be thrilled beyond imagination! There is no higher delight! I'm so thrilled to share with you this key to *happiness*, the root of peace, and the bliss of life.

Bliss, peace, and joy… such things are *yours* because they *are* Him—and He has given Himself to you!

I want to share some truths with you that might seem contrary to many things which you've heard; however, they aren't contrary at all. In fact, these truths *lie beneath* much of what you've heard.

My heart is this: that our greatest take-away from our time in ministry meetings and church settings would be that when we go home and go back to normal life, we would experience the reality of His person in our daily lives. That's the main concern. It's my focal point and life mission. Some people fall into traps because they attend powerful, Holy

Ghost-filled meetings, but then they go back to work on Monday. They change diapers on Tuesday. They are shuffling papers on Wednesday. They're working with a difficult boss or perhaps they're being tried by a tough marriage. In all these things, what we find *in Him* must stay relevant and active. We often observe the lives of great men of God and great people of stature and measure ourselves by them. It's tempting to think that what *we* have is not relevant compared to others' giftings. We think, "Well, there is no way I can pack out a stadium like so-and-so. There is no way I can minister like this person or that person. There's no way I can be as successful as them." This is perverse thinking. We must change the definition of *success* in our hearts.

Success is not miracles. Success is not preaching. Success is not people falling out in the Spirit. It's not riches and it's not fame. Do you want to know what success is? Success is a heart that is captivated by the love of Jesus.

There's a scary area of scripture where the Bible mentions how many will come to Jesus in the end saying, "Lord, Lord, did we not...?" And in essence, Jesus responds with, "You didn't have a kiss with me. You may have had public encounters, but you had no private kiss."

Oh, if you don't let Him kiss you, there's no way for you to love Him! If you've ever touched Him, you know that He has one thing on His mind in that moment: *holding you*. When you allow Him to hold you, He somehow *drains out* all of your inward poisons: bitterness, selfish ambition, anger, lusts… He drains them out when you simply let Him hold you. This, to me, is the secret of *everything*.

1

The First Mention of Mary of Bethany

"Truly I tell you, wherever this gospel is preached throughout the world, what she has done will also be told, in memory of her." Matthew 26:13 (NIV)

This means that Jesus wanted Mary of Bethany to be *remembered*. If that's true, then she must be significant! Not only that, He tied the memory of her to the global spread of the gospel! At first, this bothered me, because I thought to myself, she never preached a message. She never taught a class. She never wrote a book. She never performed any miracles. She is only mentioned three times in scripture. I said, "Lord, what could it be in this woman that would cause her to be tied to the testimony of

Your name for all time? What is it that's so special to You?"

As I waited, I heard His voice. He said, "She *loved* me." It doesn't sound significant, does it? I thought, "Lord, so many people have loved You! What makes *her* different?" I realized that God took me to this passage to show me the *kind* of love that she had, which separated her from so many others. The *kind* of love that she had was intrinsic to the spread of the gospel!

Luke 10:38, the first mention of this woman, describes her like this: "She sat at His feet, listening to His words." Isn't that beautiful? Think of this picture: a crowded house full of commotion… and then there is this woman. She is on her knees and, with fixed eyes, she is steadily staring at Him. It's the first mention of this precious woman. If I had been there, I would have been struck by her magnificent obsession. It would have hit me hard. Why? Because she didn't care what anyone thought of her. She was looking at Him. This is the life I want! To gaze upon the Lamb who was slain.

She teaches us something so significant. She teaches us that He Himself is too beautiful to look away from. She teaches us that there is actually honey dripping forth from His lips. *That* honey which drips from His lips is sweet to our taste!

> **"Gracious words are a honeycomb, sweet to the soul and healing to the bones." Proverbs 16:24 (NIV)**

> **"Know also that wisdom is like honey for you..." Proverbs 24:14 (NIV)**

I see that the story of Mary of Bethany is a call to be captivated by Him! She is a demonstration of His worth. She is a proclamation of the preeminence of His person.

Her love cries out that **He is greater than His gifts! He is more wonderful than His wonders! Stare at Him for He is greater than the anointing. He is lovely.** She wasn't standing in awe of His powers. She had found something so much more valuable. She found that He Himself was the fulfillment of her soul, the satisfaction and joy of her life. She was struck breathless by the overwhelming conviction that He is more lovely than anything she had seen. She realized that being with Him was to have everything she had ever wanted, it was to be everything she ever wanted to be, and it was to arrive everywhere she had ever dreamed of going. She found that His presence freed her from the need to have anything else. Most of all, she found that her prayers had vanished simply by His presence. How? Because she found that He was and is everything she needed and everything she ever wanted. His presence transformed the mundane and common house that she lived in into a garden of spices with her beloved. She drew near. Near enough to hear, if nothing else, His breathing.

"When the eyes of the soul looking out meet the eyes of God looking in, heaven has begun right here on earth."
—AW Tozer

Many of you might think, "I don't know this life." Let me tell you, Jesus described this life as "the good part." He went on to describe it as untouchable and eternal! Following that, He said it is "the *one thing* that is needed." In other words, "the *only* necessity in life is right here, looking at Me."

Mary shows us that the essential

Christian message is not to behave, but to behold. You can tell who doesn't *really* want God to rule their lives by who doesn't take time to simply sit and listen to Him.

The Great Contrast

Martha was too busy for the bliss and enjoyment of life with Jesus. Her relationship with Jesus was so wrapped up in what she was doing *for* Him. Oh, how easy it is to hide behind *activity!* Jesus contrasted these two sharply. One is looking at Him, the other is not. One is listening to Him, the other is not. One is near Him, the other is not. One is at rest, the other is not. Martha was simply too active to give Him her attention.

> "Activity can mask an empty soul and give a fake costume of nobility." —Martha Kilpatrick

> "Busyness can be artificial significance." —Bill Johnson

> "It is so often that our activities obstruct our union with Him." —Madame Guyon

Martha chose occupation *for* the Lord over preoccupation *with* the Lord. She wanted to feed Him, more than feed *on* Him. She preferred to be around Him than to look at Him. So many have become fixated on that which is around

Him rather than fixated on looking upon Him! It's a trap to get us to become mesmerized by His *ways* rather than His *Person*.

It's so easy to love the *flow* and forget His *face*. Oh, but there is a face that can be looked at! As we continue to look at His face, we become blinded to the things that are constantly pulling on us. This... this is called *satisfaction*. Satisfaction is not a perk of His presence. Satisfaction is the very means by which He frees you and empowers you to be able to obey Him. You have got to be kissed so you can love Him. My dear friend Michael Koulianos said to me:

"In order for my heart to love Him

constantly my heart must see Him constantly."

I know myself and how I operate, and it's probably much like you... if I don't *see* Him—I am degenerative. My mind, my eyes, my heart, my intentions and motives become degenerative. I've got to see Him! I wake up at times and put my head on the headboard and just say, "Lord, I've got to see You. I've got to see You. I worship You. I must see You!" The sweetness of God begins to flow in as the receptivity of my soul begins to open through adoration! He flows in with peace that passes all understanding. He fills my heart with joy unspeakable and full of glory. I tell you, these things are for us! In this, all the situations in our lives have no bearing on whether or not we have peace and joy. Why? Because we are mesmerized and fixed on His person! This is what Mary is trying to show us.

Martha was unable to see the real significance of having the Lord in her house. That is exactly what *activity* can do. It will rob you of your attraction to God. Martha chose to value other things rather than looking into His eyes.

"Beware the barrenness of a busy life." —Corrie Ten Boom

Martha was fruitless in this scene. The Spirit of God thought that her work was so insignificant that it wasn't even named specifically in the scriptures. Her work died with her. Yet Mary became a message to all generations connected to the gospel itself. Do you see now?

You say, "What do I do, Eric? Quit my job and move to a cave? I've got 12 kids, I'm in school, and I'm running two businesses." Allow me to define busyness to you. Busyness is *not* having a lot to do. Here is the definition of barren busyness: it is to eclipse His worth with work. It is to replace the simplicity of Christ with the multiplicity of your own ways.

"Simplicity is a loving intent upon Jesus alone, seeking no other person or thing." —John Wesley

Busyness is not having a lot to do. Jesus had a lot to do, yet it never made its way *into* Him. He remained disconnected from busyness inwardly to remain connected with His heavenly Father in the midst of everything. In this, His Father became the source of everything. Only if He is *center* can He be *source*. If He is not center, He is not source, and if He is not source, something else is! That was Martha's problem!

"Only if He is center can He be source. If He is not center, He is not source, and if He is not source — something else is!

What is dead activity? It's covering the restless, bankrupt state of your soul with things to do… things that God didn't commission. It's easy to keep outward things going while neglecting the simple act of staring into His face.

Mary shows us that He and He alone must come before all of His things. It's easy to cheat on God with stuff He gave you. When Jesus talks to Martha, He shows us that Martha's way is the source of worried, bothered, and judgmental living.

It's easy to cheat on God with stuff God gave you.

Martha eclipsed the simplicity of looking upon Him with the multiplicity of her own ways. Isn't it funny that Martha tries to diminish what Mary is doing? But notice that Mary, just like the Lamb she is beholding, offers no rebuttal! Workers always try to murder worshippers in one way or another, but to gaze at Him exposes the ones who are not gazing. Do you understand?

This choice is ever and always before you and me! We are today what we chose yesterday. We are not today what we neglected yesterday. We will be tomorrow what we elect today. The choice is yours. He has made His face completely and totally *available*.

2
The Second Mention of Mary of Bethany

Mary's brother had died. The Lord arrived at the scene and Martha actually met Him. What does she meet Him with? She talks to Him and gives Him dialogue. Her dialogue is even theological, talking about resurrection and so forth. However, in Christ's dialogue with Martha, He didn't find what He was looking for. So, the scripture says, "He looked for Mary." John 11:17-28

Words will never replace worship. He wasn't looking for someone who would throw words at Him. He wanted worship rather than words. He went looking for Mary! The first time I read this, it pierced me deeply. He sought a *worshipper*! He still does! He is looking for a "Mary" in the midst of a room. He is looking, not for mere words, but for worship in the middle of the meeting

I was at an event in which prayers and outcries were being offered profusely to the Lord. In the midst of the meeting, I was taken up in a vision, and as I overlooked the room, I saw that all of the prayers going up were all one specific color. However, there was one person who had prayers going up that were a different color than all of the rest. In the vision, I was able to hone in on the one person's prayer, and as I leaned in, I heard the person saying, "You, You, You! I want You, oh Lord!" The Lord wants us to sanctify His name. He desires that His name be lifted up and picked up higher and higher than the rest—because He is more lovely and beautiful. He will literally blind us to everything else. Our simple adoration and desire for Him and Him alone sets our prayers apart from mere petition.

So here in the story, Mary comes to Jesus. Her brother has died. Her heart is hurting and she doesn't understand. What does she do? She throws herself at His feet. Can you see why she was so *special* to Him? Everyone else is standing up and talking. They have opinions about this and that and plenty of unanswered questions. Yet what does Mary do? She throws everything and herself at His feet. An act that professes, "You, Lord, are more lovely and worthy to me than all the answers and facts that I could find!"

Here is the problem: men would rather *explain* than *adore*. They would rather inquire than simply adore. Mary shows us that she is willing to worship Him despite not understanding. Certainly she had feelings and thoughts and questions about the situation—yet she was willing to throw them down, along with her own life, at the feet of Jesus. She is literally saying that Christ's *presence* is more important than *answers*.

I don't know what you're going through or what you've been through, but I know that He *Himself* is better than any answer He could give you. Too often we get distracted by what He gives and we begin to come to Him for something other than *Him*... and we wonder why we keep missing the sweet, blissful enjoyment of His person!

Even though Mary and Martha had similar discussions with Jesus, He responded with resurrection power to Mary only. Do you see this? Mary shows us that she would rather *move* Him than *understand* Him. She was more interested in *touching* Him than *defining* Him. She shows us that something takes place in adoration that makes understanding not that important anymore. The memory of her, which is intrinsic to the gospel, is God's invitation for all to love Him as she loved Him. She is the embodiment of the first commandment.

"Mary shows us that she would rather move Him than understand Him. She was more interested in touching Him than defining Him.

Mary is the lovesick one. She is sick with love. In fact, she has symptoms of lovesickness. The primary symptom is a fixed gaze that cannot look away or be broken. I pray that you would become so lovesick that you would have this same problem. In this, no matter what other people do to you or against you, it matters not, because you'd have to take your eyes off of Him to see them anyway… and you can't.

3

The Third Mention of Mary of Bethany

The final time Mary is mentioned, she is again blinded by her surroundings. She takes a very costly vial of perfume and breaks it over His feet and dries His feet with her hair. She poured it all out. Every last drop was given. She didn't merely pour out part of the perfume. Why? Because He was *all* to her. What you give to Him and *how much* you give to Him and what you hold back are all measurements of the condition of your love for Him. As she pours out the entire vial of perfume, the purity of her love causes a rise of the impurity in Judas. Did you notice this? He says, "Why wasn't this perfume sold and the money given to the poor?" (John 12:5, NIV).

This shows me that Mary scandalizes all those who love the work of the Lord more than the Lord of the work. It shows me that the purity of *only* wanting Him exposes the impurity of merely wanting something from Him.

"

This shows me that Mary scandalizes all those who love the work of the Lord more than the Lord of the work.

Jesus said, "The poor you will always have with you, but you will not always have me." Matthew 26:11 (NIV) In other words, someone better than *good things* is here! In your life, someone greater than good things is here!

Here is the wild part: when she breaks the perfume on His feet and wipes it with her hair, she smells like Him and He smells like her! Such is the life that is lived in loving adoration of the Lord! The scripture says that the whole house was filled with the fragrance. In essence, their sweet, loving, personal intimacy affected everyone around them. So it will be with you, if you choose to set your gaze, fix your heart, and lived wrapped in His presence!

Mary hit the gospel on the head with the

understanding that God wants to mix with man. She hit the target with a revelation that God wants you to become the message and not just carry one! Sweet adoration was their mingling. Maybe this is why Paul said, "to the one an aroma from death to death, to the other an aroma from life to life" (2 Corinthians 2:16).

And so, an ordinary woman who never wrote a book, preached a sermon, or performed miracles stole the heart of Jesus. She shows us what the gospel is supposed to bring everyone to: the feet of the Lord. My desire is that grace for adoration would come upon you. I pray that a rock would be struck in your heart and a flow of adoration would spring forth. That it would change the way you wash dishes, change diapers, travel on airplanes, sit in meetings, drive down the street, and counsel and teach. That you would be erupting inside with the sweet, empowering presence of Jesus.

A Closing Story

Once when I was freshly born-again, a man came to pick me up for a road trip. He got in the car and looked at me and said, "Let's pray." As a response, I began shooting off in tongues and praying with all of my might. I didn't know what else to do; it was what I had *seen*. I was mimicking what I had beheld. This man waited for me to get tired, because he knew it would happen at some point. He waited for the smoke to clear from my all out assault on hell. With a steaming coffee in one hand and a steering wheel in the other, he simply said softly, "Jesus… I worship you. There is no one like You. I worship You."

I began tearing up. God's presence filled the car. At the same time, I was so frustrated with how easily he touched God. I learned something that day that stayed with me forever: one ounce of adoration is worth tons and tons of effort and striving.

If I could sum up this entire message with a single phrase that I pray you wouldn't forget, it would be this: ***snuggle* don't *struggle*.**

ALSO FROM ERIC GILMOUR

The School of His Presence

Burn

Union

How to Prosper in Everything

Enjoying the Gospel

Into the Cloud

Nostalgia

ABOUT THE AUTHOR

Eric William Gilmour is the founder of Sonship International - a ministry seeking to bring the church into a deeper experience of God's presence in their daily lives. He enjoys writing on the revelation of Jesus Christ in the Scriptures and personal experience of God.

For More Information & Resources:

Sonship International
P. O. Box 196281
Winter Springs, Fl.32719

sonship-international.org

Eric William Gilmour

**PULPIT
TO PAGE
PUBLISHING**

Made in the USA
Lexington, KY
31 May 2018